THE LIBRARY OF PHYSICAL SCIENCE™

States of Matter

Suzanne Slade

The Rosen Publishing Group's

PowerKids Press™

New York

To Brooke and Freddy Buckingham

Published in 2007 by The Rosen Publishing Group, Inc.
29 East 21st Street, New York, NY 10010

First Edition

Editors: Melissa Acevedo and Amelie von Zumbusch
Book Design: Elana Davidian
Layout Design: Ginny Chu
Photo Researcher: Gabriel Caplan

Photo Credits: Cover © Mehau Kulyk/Photo Researchers, Inc.; p. 4 © Digital Vision; pp. 5, 10 © Photodisc; p. 6 © Mark Garlick/Photo Researchers, Inc.; p. 7 © Scott Camazine/Photo Researchers, Inc.; p. 8 © Gusto/Photo Researchers, Inc.; p. 9 © Aaron Haupt/Photo Researchers, Inc.; p. 11 © Corbis/Punchstock; p. 12 © Ellen B. Senisi/The Image Works; p. 13 © Andrew Lambert Photography/Photo Researchers, Inc.; p. 14 © David McNew/Getty Images; p. 15 © David Young-Wolff/Photo Edit; p. 16 © Daniel Smith/zefa/Corbis; p. 17 © StockFood/Imrie; p. 18 © Martyn F. Chillmaid/Photo Researchers, Inc.; p. 19 © Clive Freeman/Biosym Technologies/Photo Researchers, Inc.; p. 20 © David Parker/Photo Researchers, Inc.; p. 21 © Custom Medical Stock Photo.

Library of Congress Cataloging-in-Publication Data

Slade, Suzanne.
  States of matter / Suzanne Slade.— 1st ed.
      p. cm. — (The library of physical science)
  Includes index.
  ISBN 1-4042-3416-0 (lib. bdg.) — ISBN 1-4042-2163-8 (pbk.)
  1. Matter—Properties—Juvenile literature. 2. Atoms—Juvenile literature. 3. Molecular—Juvenile literature. I. Title. II. Series.
  QC173.36.S42 2007
  530.4—dc22
                                        2005028071

Manufactured in the United States of America

Contents

Defining Matter

Matter is all around you. It is everywhere you look. The computer on your desk, your favorite soda, the air you breathe, and even your pet hamster are made up of matter. Scientists use the word "matter" to mean anything that takes up space.

Everything on Earth is made of matter. Can you find examples of different kinds of matter in the picture above?

Earth and the Moon, seen here from space, are both made of matter.

Matter comes in several different states. It can be solid, like a telephone. Matter can also be liquid, like the water in a fish bowl. Some matter is in the form of a gas. For example, the **helium** in a balloon, which makes it float, is a colorless gas.

Every **planet** in the **universe** has matter. Everything in the world, from the tallest mountain to the deepest ocean, is made of matter. Matter makes up your skin, eyes, hair, and the rest of your body. Wherever you go and whatever you do, matter always surrounds you!

How Matter Is Formed

Matter is made of tiny **particles** called **atoms**. Every solid, liquid, and gas in the universe has atoms. Atoms are so small you cannot see them.

Atoms consist of three parts. These parts are protons, neutrons, and electrons. The

The purple and green neutrons and protons make up the nucleus of this atom. The electrons are the pink balls spinning around the nucleus.

nucleus is in the center of an atom. It is made of protons and neutrons. A neutron has no electric charge. Neutrons surround the positively charged protons and keep them from pushing

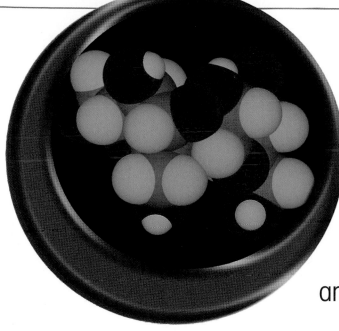

Sucrose molecules, like the one above, have three different types of atoms. Sucrose is another name for table sugar.

away from each other. Electrons, which are **negatively** charged, move around the nucleus. The electric charges of these three parts help hold an atom together.

Atoms join to form **molecules**. Some molecules, like table salt, are made of only two atoms. Other molecules are larger. For example, a sugar molecule has 45 atoms. Some molecules have many different sorts of atoms. Other molecules have only one kind of atom. Elements are kinds of matter with only one type of atom.

Physical Properties of Matter

Different kinds of matter have different **physical** properties. Physical properties are things you observe or measure, like size, shape, color, feel, smell, and taste. Some physical properties you can measure are the **temperatures** at which matter boils, **freezes**, or melts. You can recognize matter by its physical properties. For example, if a friend gives you a present that is thin, hard, and rectangular, and that smells like chocolate, you know it is a chocolate bar.

Physical properties, like color and smell, allow you to recognize chocolate.

The bowling ball, at left, and the balloon, shown below, are the same size. The bowling ball has a higher density because its molecules are more tightly packed.

Mass is an important physical property of matter. The amount of matter in an object is its mass. The mass of an object does not change. Volume is a physical property that tells you how much space a certain object takes up. Scientists use mass and volume to find the **density** of matter. Density tells you how tightly packed molecules are in matter. To find an object's density, you **divide** its mass by its volume.

Solids

Solids are one of the three most common states of matter. Solids are hard and can keep their shape. Your home, books, and toys are all solid matter.

Molecules stick tightly to each other in solids. Solids cannot change their own shape because their molecules cannot move much. People can change the shape of some solids. When you break a stick into two pieces, you change its shape. The volume of solids stays the

Even if you cut up a pickle, its volume will always stay the same.

These marbles are solid. They cannot change shape to fill a jar. They leave empty space between themselves.

same. The two smaller stick pieces take up the same amount of space as the original stick did.

The molecules in a solid are tightly packed together. The density of a solid does not change. For example, you know your computer will keep its shape and not become soft or drip off your desk.

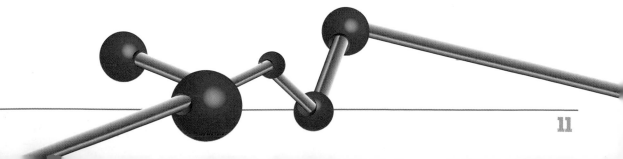

Liquids

Liquids are another common state of matter. Liquids do not have a shape of their own, and they can move and flow. Some liquids, like lemonade, move easily. Other liquids, like maple syrup, move slowly. Maple syrup is a thick, sweet liquid made from the sap of maple trees.

Water is an important liquid. You need to drink water every day because your body is made

You can pour liquids, such as orange juice. This is because the molecules in a liquid slide over each other easily.

These glasses hold the same volume of orange juice, even though their shapes are different.

mostly of water. Water is also used to clean things, such as your clothes and dishes. Many liquids you drink, such as milk, juice, and soda, have water in them.

The molecules in a liquid are not stuck together. Liquid molecules move and take the shape of any **container**. Even though a liquid's shape may change, its volume does not. For example, if you pour a can of soda into a tall, thin glass, the soda's volume remains the same. The only difference is that this liquid has a different shape.

Gases

The third common state of matter is gas. Like liquids, gases do not have a certain shape. A gas can change its shape to fit the container in which it is placed.

Gases are used for many things. You breathe in oxygen gas and breathe out carbon dioxide gas. Some houses use natural gas for cooking and heating. Gases such as nitrogen and ammonia are used to make fertilizer. Farmers use fertilizer to help crops grow.

The molecules in a gas are always moving. Gas molecules bump off each other and the walls of the container that holds them. The density of a gas can

You cannot see natural gas, but you can see the flames it makes when it burns.

You breathe out the gases carbon dioxide and water vapor. Water vapor is water in the form of a gas.

change. If you pop a helium balloon, the helium molecules will spread out in the room. The density, or how close together the helium molecules are, will go down. The density of a gas goes up if a gas is moved from a large container to a smaller one.

Changing States of Matter

Matter can change from one state to another. For example, a solid ice cube can change into water. Water can also turn into a gas, called water vapor. Temperature changes can cause matter to change state. Water becomes a solid when its temperature drops below 32° F (0° C). Water turns into gas when its temperature is raised until it boils. Matter can also change state when its **pressure** changes. Propane gas, which is used in gas grills, becomes a liquid when it is pressed into a container. The pressure in the tank

If it becomes warm enough, a solid ice cube will melt into a liquid puddle of water.

Chocolate becomes liquid when you melt it. Then you can pour it on ice cream!

pushes the gas molecules together until they form a liquid.

When matter changes state, its physical properties change. This allows matter to be used in different ways. For example, when solid chocolate melts, you can pour it on ice cream. Matter can change back to its original state. Melted chocolate will become solid again when it cools.

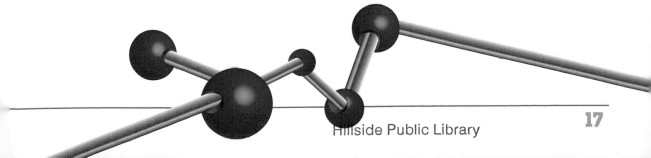

The Kinetic Theory of Matter

All matter is made of tiny particles. Scientists think that the particles in matter are always moving. This idea is called the **kinetic theory** of matter.

Particles in a solid are close together. They vibrate, or move back and forth, a very small amount. You cannot feel it, but the particles in this book are vibrating. The particles in liquids are usually farther apart than are particles in solids. Liquid particles can move away from

When water boils, its molecules begin to move so quickly that they become a gas.

These water molecules are evaporating. This means the fastest-moving molecules are breaking loose and becoming the gas water vapor.

each other. Particles in gases have an even greater distance between them. They move very fast and fill empty spaces near them. Some air molecules travel faster than 1,800 miles per hour (2,897 km/h)!

When matter is heated, its particles move faster. The higher the temperature, the faster the molecules travel. Different types of matter have different-sized particles. Lighter particles move faster than heavy particles.

Scientific Instruments Used to Study Matter

Most types of matter, such as solids and liquids, are easy to see and observe. Some gases, like oxygen and helium, cannot be seen. Nor can you see the atoms that make up all matter. This is because atoms are too small to see. Scientists need special instruments to look at and study these tiny pieces of matter.

Scientists use certain kinds of **microscopes** to see atoms. Electron microscopes show scientists how atoms are arranged in matter. Another

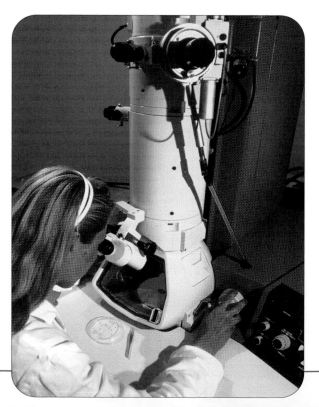

This scientist is using an electron microscope to study matter.

Scientists use many kinds of balances to measure mass. This balance shows pieces of aluminum (left) and lead (right) that have the same mass.

microscope, called a scanning tunneling microscope, shows the shape and surface of atoms. These microscopes help scientists learn about atoms.

Scientists use a balance to measure the amount of mass in a certain piece of matter. The first step in using a balance is to zero the scale. To do this scientists place an empty cup on the balance and set the scale to zero. Next matter is placed in the cup, and the balance will show the amount of mass.

Other States of Matter

Solids, liquids, and gases are the three most common states of matter. However, scientists have also discovered other kinds of matter. Plasma is a state of matter found at very high temperatures or low pressures. Plasma conducts electricity. Flat TV screens use plasmas. Another type of matter, Bose-Einstein condensate, was discovered in 1995. BEC, as it is known, forms at the coldest temperature scientists can create. Atoms placed in this temperature form one large BEC atom. BEC lasts for only a few minutes.

You use all kinds of matter. You need solid food to eat, air to breathe, and water to drink. New discoveries about matter will help the people of tomorrow.

Glossary

atoms (A-temz) The smallest parts of elements that can exist either alone or with other elements.

container (kun-TAY-ner) Something that holds things.

density (DEN-seh-tee) The heaviness of an object compared to its size.

divide (dih-VYD) To find out the number of times one number goes into another number.

freezes (FREEZ-ez) Makes something so cold it becomes solid.

helium (HEE-lee-um) A light colorless gas.

kinetic theory (kuh-NEH-tik THEE-uh-ree) The idea that the particles in matter are always moving.

microscopes (MY-kruh-skohps) Instruments used to see very small things.

molecules (MAH-lih-kyoolz) Two or more atoms joined together.

negatively (NEH-guh-tiv-lee) The opposite of positively.

particles (PAR-tih-kulz) Small pieces of matter.

physical (FIH-zih-kul) Having to do with natural forces.

planet (PLA-net) A large object, such as Earth, that moves around the Sun.

pressure (PREH-shur) A force that pushes on something.

temperatures (TEM-pur-cherz) How hot or cold things are.

universe (YOO-nih-vers) All of space.

Index

Web Sites

Due to the changing nature of Internet links, PowerKids Press has developed an online list of Web sites related to the subject of this book. This site is updated regularly. Please use this link to access the list:
www.powerkidslinks.com/lops/matter/